Introduction

contents contents

Chocolate

Chocolate casts a magical spell. It has melted in the hands of fresh-faced children, adorned the wedding cakes at even the finest royal banquets and has been blamed for the downfall of many a woman chasing the fantasy of the perfect physique. Love it or hate it, chocolate has become one of the world's most sought-after luxuries.

In the eighteenth century, a Swedish naturalist named Carolus Linneaus, creator of the modern system of naming all living things, dubbed the tree from which chocolate comes, Cacao theobroma;

cacao meaning 'food of the gods'. It was believed that emperor Montezuma drank nothing else but a cold, bitter concoction of chocolate, flavoured with spices, and prepared to the consistency of honey. Belief that chocolate is an aphrodisiac originated from his ritual of drinking chocolate in a goblet before entering his harem. Entrenched in such an intriguing period of history, it is easy to see why romantic notions surrounding chocolate have persisted and made this exquisite delicacy one of the most prevalent gifts for lovers on St Valentine's Day.

Although some history books state that famous explorer Christopher Columbus brought back cacao beans to King Ferdinand of Spain from his fourth visit to the New World, their cultural and commercial value was eclipsed by the king's interest in other spoils of his adventures afar. It was only with Spanish explorer Hernando Cortez's visit to the court of Montezuma in the 1500s that a more defined interest in this drinkable delicacy was noted.

Despite their links to South America, most of the world's cacao beans today come from West Africa, with Ghana, Nigeria and the Ivory Coast as the prime producers. It is believed that the change in name to cocoa was the result of a spelling error made by English traders.

introduction

The cross over from ancient ritual to modern day delight was made when the chocolate beverage became a fashionable social event at the first chocolate house in London in the mid 1600s. Unlike today, it was the domain of the elite because of its hefty price. Since the cocoa bean became a form of trading currency in many nations, to drink chocolate was like drinking money. It was only with the improvements in transportation from plantation to factory and the advent of the Industrial Revolution that the production of chocolate made it more accessible to the masses.

Chocolate was introduced to the United States in the mid 1700s as an import from the West Indies, but it failed to become fully accepted by the colonists until fishermen from Massachusetts accepted cocoa beans as payment for cargo. Originally, the chocolate drink was predominantly enjoyed by men but eventually gained a more widespread, socially acceptable patronage among women and children. It had many additions, including milk, wine, beer or spices, and at one stage was even regarded as having medicinal qualities by leading physicians.

To make eating chocolate, the fruit from the cacao tree is picked, their pods opened and the beans removed. These beans are fermented, dried, cleaned, roasted and hulled. Once the shells are removed, they are given the term, nibs. These nibs are blended to produce different colors and flavors, much like coffee. The grinding process releases the cocoa butter, and the heat from this process causes the extracted cocoa butter and finely-ground nibs to melt together. This creates the fluid chocolate liquor that forms the basis of countless chocolate varieties all over the globe.

There has been an obvious evolution from basic use to more advanced preparation procedures. Unprocessed chocolate is unsuitable for eating because of its rough, gritty texture. It was only with Swiss chocolate manufacturer Rudolph Lindt, for which the famous brand is named, that the process of rolling and kneading chocolate to give it a smoother texture was discovered. This process was known as conching because of the shell-like shape of the rollers used in the process. The more chocolate and its additives are conched, the smoother and more luxurious it tastes to the palate.

Cooking with chocolate is a journey into seventh heaven. From luscious mud cake to mouth-watering mousse, chocolate forms the basis for many delectable desserts. Its rich flavour provides a gratifying taste experience and its deep, brown colour and numerous applications deliver a visual appeal unequalled by any other cooking ingredient. No wonder chocolate has stood the test of centuries.

But often labelled as a wicked temptation for the health conscious to avoid at all costs, only in recent years have the health benefits of chocolate emerged. Scientific tests have found that chocolate contains several vitamins including B1, B2, D, and E. In addition, there are schools of thought that claim some of the substances found in chocolate actually release endorphins, which provide a pleasurable sensation and further add to its irresistibility. Maybe Montezuma had it right after all…

a piece
of cake

sticky chocolate

and raspberry slice

85g/3oz unsalted butter, plus extra for greasing

85g/3oz plain chocolate, broken into chunks

85g/3oz fresh or frozen raspberries, defrosted if frozen, plus extra to decorate

2 medium eggs, separated

55g/2oz powder sugar

30g/1oz ground almonds

30g/1oz cocoa powder, sifted

30g/1oz plain flour, sifted

confectioners sugar to dust and fresh mint to decorate

For the sauce

145g/5oz fresh or frozen raspberries, defrosted if frozen

1 tbsp powder sugar (optional)

1 Preheat the oven to 180°C/350°F/Gas Mark 4. Grease the base and sides of an 18cm/7in loose-bottomed cake tin and line with baking paper. Melt the chocolate and butter in a bowl set over a saucepan of simmering water, stirring. Cool slightly.

2 Meanwhile, press 85g/3oz raspberries through a sieve. Whisk the egg yolks and sugar until pale and creamy, then mix in the almonds, cocoa, flour, melted chocolate and sieved raspberries.

3 Whisk the egg whites until they form stiff peaks (this is best done with an electric whisk). Fold a little into the chocolate mixture to loosen, then fold in the remainder. Spoon into the tin and cook for 25 minutes or until risen and just firm. Cool for 1 hour.

4 For the sauce, sieve the raspberries, then stir in the sugar, if using. Remove the cake from the tin and dust with the confectioners sugar. Serve with the sauce, decorated with mint and raspberries.

7

mini chocolate muffins
with mocha sauce

1 Preheat the oven to 180°C/350°F/Gas Mark 4. Grease a 12-hole muffin tray. Melt the chocolate and butter in a bowl set over a saucepan of simmering water. Place the eggs, sugar, flour and cocoa powder into a bowl and beat for 1 minute, then beat in the melted chocolate and butter.

2 Spoon into the muffin tray, allowing 1 tablespoon for each hole. Bake for 15 minutes or until risen and firm to the touch.

3 Meanwhile, make the mocha sauce. Place the chocolate, coffee and 55mL/2fl oz of cream into a small pan and heat gently. Simmer for 1-2 minutes, until the sauce has thickened slightly. Keep warm.

4 Allow the muffins to cool on a wire rack for 5 minutes. Whisk the remaining cream until thickened, then spoon over the muffins together with the mocha sauce. Serve dusted with cocoa powder.

Note: You'll need a 12-hole, non-stick muffin tray for these mini muffins or, if you prefer, you can make large muffins and increase the cooking time to 25 minutes.

55g/2oz unsalted butter, diced, plus extra for greasing

55g/2oz plain chocolate, broken into pieces

2 medium eggs

75g/3½oz powder sugar

75g/3½oz self-raising flour

25g/1oz cocoa powder, sifted, plus extra for dusting

For the mocha sauce

145g/5oz plain chocolate, broken into pieces

85mL/3fl oz espresso or other strong, good quality coffee

145mL/5oz carton double cream

Makes 12 **Preparation** 10mins plus 5mins cooling
Cooking 15mins **Calories** 160 **Fat** 11g

chocolate

cheesecake

1 To make the base, place the biscuits into a plastic bag, seal, then crush with a rolling pin to make crumbs. Place in a large bowl, then mix in the butter and sugar. Add the cinnamon, if using, and mix again. Press the mixture evenly into the base and up the sides of a 23cm/9in loose-bottomed flan tin. Refrigerate until needed.

2 Preheat the oven to 180°C/350°F/Gas Mark 4. In a large bowl, beat the soft cheese with a wooden spoon until soft and fluffy. Lightly beat the eggs in a small bowl, then gradually beat into the soft cheese with the sugar. Stir until the mixture is smooth. Set aside.

3 Melt the chocolate in a small bowl set over a saucepan of simmering water, stirring frequently. Remove from the heat and stir in the soured cream and the rum, if using. Mix well.

4 Stir the chocolate mixture into the cheese mixture, then pour over the biscuit base. Bake for 30 minutes or until the edges of the mixture look set (the middle may still look moist). Turn the heat off, and leave the cheesecake to cool for 1 hour in the oven, with the door open.

5 Place the cheesecake in the fridge for 2 hours. If using the strawberries, arrange them around the edge of the cheesecake before serving.

For the base

200g/7oz low-fat digestive biscuits

100g/3½oz unsalted butter, at room temperature

1 tbsp sugar

¼ tsp ground cinnamon (optional)

For the filling

400g/14oz full-fat soft cheese, at room temperature

2 eggs

145g/5oz powder sugar

200g/7oz dark chocolate, broken into pieces

145mL/5fl oz carton soured cream

1 tbsp dark rum (optional)

115g/4oz strawberries, halved, to decorate (optional)

Serves 8   **Preparation** 30mins plus 1hr cooling and 2hrs setting
Cooking 30mins   **Calories** 635 **Fat** 41g

simple chocolate

For the cake

1 tsp sunflower oil for greasing

125g/4½oz plain flour, plus 2 tsp for flouring

30g/1oz cocoa powder

2 tsp baking powder

125g/4½oz powder sugar

2 large eggs, lightly beaten

125g/4½oz soft margarine

3 tbsp milk

For the filling

145mL/5fl oz carton double cream

2 tbsp raspberry jam

1 tbsp confectioners sugar to dust

1 Preheat the oven to 180°C/350°/Gas Mark 4. Grease two 18cm/7in sandwich tins with the oil, using a pastry brush or a folded sheet of kitchen towel. Add a teaspoon of flour to each tin, then tilt the tin and knock the sides so that the flour covers the inside. Tip out any excess.

2 Sift the flour, cocoa powder and baking powder into a bowl, add the sugar, eggs, margarine and milk. Beat with a wooden spoon or an electric whisk until the mixture is soft and smooth.

3 Using a large metal spoon, divide the mixture between the two tins, spreading evenly. Bake for 25 minutes, until the tops are firm and springy. To check the cakes are cooked, insert a knife or skewer into the middle of one – it should come out clean. If the knife is sticky, bake for 5 minutes more and test again. Leave to cool in the tins for 10 minutes.

4 To remove each cake from its tin, loosen the sides with a knife, then place a large plate over the top and flip the cake over. Cool the cakes, right-side up, on a wire rack.

5 For the filling, whisk the cream until it forms soft peaks. Spread one cake with the raspberry jam, and top with the cream. Place the other cake on top. Just before serving, place the icing sugar in a sieve and tap lightly to dust the cakes with sugar.

Serves 6 ***Preparation*** *20mins + 30mins cooling*
Cooking *30mins* ***Calories*** *479* ***Fat*** *31g*

cake

chocolate and

strawberry roulade

sunflower spread for greasing	15g/¹/₂oz cocoa powder, sifted, plus 2 tsp to dust
3 medium eggs	125g/4¹/₂oz Greek yoghurt
125g/4¹/₂oz powdered sugar	100g/3¹/₂oz virtually fat-free fromage frais
55g/2oz plain wholemeal flour	145g/5oz strawberries, sliced or chopped
55g/2oz plain flour, sifted	confectioners sugar to dust

1 Preheat the oven to 200°C/ 400°F/Gas Mark 6. Grease a 33x23cm/13x9in swiss roll tin and line with non- stick baking paper. Place the eggs and sugar into a heatproof bowl over a saucepan of simmering water and whisk until pale and creamy. Remove from the heat and whisk until cool.

2 Lightly fold the wholemeal flour into the mixture using a metal spoon, then fold in the plain flour and cocoa powder with 1 tablespoon of hot water. Pour into the tin and smooth the surface with the back of a spoon.

3 Bake for 10-12 minutes, until risen and firm. Turn out onto a sheet of non-stick baking paper, trim the edges of the sponge with a sharp knife and roll up with the paper inside. Place seam-side down on a wire rack and leave to cool for 30 minutes, then carefully unroll and discard the paper.

4 Mix together the Greek yoghurt and fromage frais and spread evenly over the cake. Scatter over the strawberries, then roll up the cake. Dust with cocoa powder and confectioners sugar.

Note: Fromage fraise is strawberry cream cheese, normally available from your favourite delicatessen.

rich dark
chocolate

400g/14oz unsalted butter, plus greasing

5 x 100g/3½oz packs luxury continental chocolate, broken into pieces

350g/12½oz powder sugar

6 tbsp plain flour

6 large eggs, separated

pinch of salt

For the coating

6 tbsp seedless raspberry jelly or cherry preserve

2 x 100g/3½oz packs luxury continental chocolate, broken into pieces

4 tbsp single cream

2 tbsp confectioners sugar

raspberries and fresh mint to decorate (optional)

1 Preheat the oven to 200°C/400°F/Gas Mark 6. Butter 2 x 900g/2lb loaf tins. Melt the chocolate with 3 tablespoons water, the butter and sugar in a bowl set over a saucepan of simmering water. Sift in the flour and stir, then beat in the egg yolks.

2 Place the egg whites into a bowl with a pinch of salt. Whisk until the mixture forms stiff peaks (this is easiest with an electric whisk). Fold 1 tablespoon of the whites into the chocolate mixture to loosen it, then fold in the remaining whites.

3 Divide the mixture between the tins and tap on the work surface to settle the contents. Bake for 45 minutes or until firm. Cool for 15 minutes in the tins. Turn out onto a cooling rack and leave for 2 hours or until cooled completely.

4 For the coating, melt the jelly with 3 tablespoons of water in a pan. Brush over the tops and sides of the cakes. Melt the chocolate with 3 tablespoons of water in a bowl set over a pan of simmering water, then stir in the cream and sugar. Smooth over the top and sides of the cakes, then place in the fridge for 1 hour. Decorate with raspberries and mint, if using.

Serves 20 **Preparation** 30mins plus 2hrs 15mins cooling and 1hr chilling
Cooking 50mins **Calories** 488 **Fat** 32g

cake

creamy

chocolate cheesecake

100g/3¹/₂oz low-fat digestive biscuits

55g/2oz butter

1 tbsp golden syrup

200g/7oz cream cheese

2 tbsp powder sugar

100g/3¹/₂oz plain chocolate drops

25g/1oz cocoa powder, sifted

200mL/7fl oz whipping or double cream

30g/1oz plain chocolate, shaved with a vegetable peeler, to decorate

1 Preheat the oven to 180°C/350°F/Gas Mark 4. Place the biscuits into a plastic bag and crush with a rolling pin. Gently heat the butter and syrup until melted, stirring. Mix in the biscuits, then pack into an 18cm/7in loose-bottomed cake tin and cook for 15 minutes or until crisp. Cool for 20 minutes.

2 Beat the cream cheese with the sugar until soft. Melt half the chocolate drops in a bowl set over a saucepan of simmering water. Blend the cocoa to a paste with 2 tablespoons of boiling water. Stir it into the melted chocolate and then fold in the cream cheese mixture. Stir in the remaining chocolate drops.

3 Whip 100mL/3¹/₂fl oz of the cream until it forms soft peaks. Fold it into the chocolate mixture, then spoon over the biscuit base. Refrigerate for 2 hours or until set. Remove from the tin. Whip the remaining cream and spread over the cheesecake and top with the chocolate shavings.

Serves 8   **Preparation** *35mins plus 20mins cooling & 2hrs chilling*   **Cooking** *15mins*
Calories *387*   **Fat** *30g*

mousse
and puddings

ice-cream

with hot chocolate sauce

30g/1oz cocoa powder, sifted

55g/2oz soft light or dark brown sugar

30g/1oz butter

1 tbsp golden syrup

4 servings vanilla ice cream

1 Place the cocoa powder and 385mL/10fl oz boiling water in a small saucepan, stir to combine, then gently bring to the boil. Reduce the heat and simmer for 10 minutes or until reduced by about three-quarters, whisking from time to time.

2 Stir in the sugar, butter and golden syrup and cook gently for 2-3 minutes, until the sugar and butter have melted and the sauce looks shiny.

3 Place the ice cream into 4 bowls. Pour over the hot chocolate sauce and serve straight away.

Note: This chocolate sauce is made with cocoa powder, but it has such a rich, scrumptious flavour that you'd think it was made from the best-quality chocolate and nothing else!

Serves 4   **Preparation** 5mins   **Cooking** 15mins   **Calories** 291   **Fat** 15g

chocolate

unsalted butter for greasing

2x100g/3¹/₂oz bars luxury continental chocolate, broken into pieces

1 tsp ground ginger

1 tsp natural vanilla extract

4 large eggs, separated

145g/5oz powder sugar

2 tbsp plain flour

¹/₂ teaspoon baking powder

confectioners sugar for dusting

For the ginger cream

285mL/10fl oz carton whipping cream

1 tbsp chilled ginger cordial

1 tsp ground ginger

confectioners sugar to taste

Serves 6
Preparation 20mins plus 20 mins chilling
Cooking 20mins
Calories 536   **Fat** 35g

1 Butter 6x10cm/2 x 4in ovenproof soufflé dishes. Refrigerate for 20 minutes. Place the chocolate in a bowl set over a pan of simmering water. Stir until melted, then stir in the ginger and vanilla extract.

2 Preheat the oven to 190°C/375°F/Gas Mark 5. Remove the soufflé dishes from the refrigerator and butter again. Whisk the egg yolks into the chocolate mixture, then fold in the sugar and flour with a metal spoon. Whisk the egg whites until stiff (this is easiest with an electric whisk). Fold a spoonful into the mixture to loosen it, then fold in the remainder. Spoon the mixture into the dishes and cook for 20 minutes or until well risen.

3 Meanwhile, make the ginger cream. Whip the cream until it forms soft peaks. Fold in the ginger cordial and ground ginger and sweeten to taste with icing sugar. Dust the puddings with confectioners sugar and serve warm with the ginger cream.

100g/3½oz plain chocolate, broken into pieces

200mL/7oz carton crème fraîche

4 tbsp natural yoghurt

finely grated rind of 1 orange

145g/5oz low-fat digestive biscuits

2 x 312g/11oz cans mandarin segments, drained

mandarin

and chocolate layers

1 Melt the chocolate in a bowl placed over a pan of simmering water, then leave to cool for 5 minutes. Add the crème fraîche, yoghurt and orange rind, reserving a few strips for decoration, to the chocolate and mix together well.

2 Place the biscuits into a plastic bag and roughly crush with a rolling pin. Divide half the crushed biscuits between 4 dessert glasses, then top with a layer of the chocolate mixture.

3 Spoon in the mandarins, reserving a few for decoration, then sprinkle the remaining crushed biscuits over them. Top with the remaining chocolate mixture and the reserved mandarins and decorate with the orange rind.

Serves 4   *Preparation* 15mins plus 5mins cooling
Cooking 5 mins   *Calories* 390   *Fat* 33g

chocolate

and orange mousse

1 tbsp arrowroot

400mL/14fl oz
orange juice

grated rind of 1 orange

3 tbsp powder sugar

2 x 100g/3½oz bars luxury
continental chocolate,
broken into pieces

2-3 tbsp orange liqueur
or brandy

butter for greasing

145mL/5fl oz carton
whipping cream

145mL/5fl oz carton
double cream

fresh strawberries
to decorate

1 Mix together the arrowroot and 3 tablespoons of the orange juice until smooth. Place the rest of the orange juice, the rind and sugar in a small saucepan and bring to the boil, then simmer for 1 minute or until the sugar has dissolved. Stir in the arrowroot mixture and bring back to the boil, stirring constantly. Boil for a few seconds, stirring, until the mixture is glossy and slightly thickened.

2 Add the chocolate to the orange mixture, then remove from the heat and stir until the chocolate has melted. Stir in the liqueur, then cover the mixture with a round of buttered baking paper to prevent a skin forming. Cool for 30 minutes.

3 Whip the whipping and double cream until the mixture forms soft peaks. Gently fold into the cooled chocolate mixture. Transfer to serving dishes, cover and place in the fridge for 2 hours. Remove from the fridge 15 minutes before serving and decorate with strawberries.

Serves *6* ***Preparation*** *15mins plus 30mins cooling and 2hrs chilling*
Cooking *5mins* ***Calories*** *461* ***Fat*** *33g*

chocolate
cream brûlee

1 Cut the plum pudding into tiny cubes and sprinkle some pudding cubes equally among the bases of each of 12 oven-proof ramekins.

2 Place a large stainless steel bowl over a pot of simmering water and whisk the cream and sugar together gently (over the simmering water) until the sugar has dissolved. Add the chocolate, broken into small pieces, and continue mixing until the chocolate has dissolved. Remove from the heat.

3 In a separate bowl, whisk the egg yolks until they form a smooth 'ribbon. Mix the whisked egg yolks, chocolate mixture and Dutch cocoa until thoroughly combined. Pour this custard mixture into a jug and divide between the prepared ramekins.

4 Place the ramekins into a large oven-proof baking dish and add hot water to reach halfway up the outsides. Bake at 150°C/300°F for 30 minutes (or until set). Remove the baking dish and take the ramekins out of the water bath. Chill the custards for at least 2 hours (or overnight).

5 Before serving, sieve the confectioners sugar generously over the custards. Caramelise the sugar under a grill until bubbling and golden. Alternatively, for a bit of fun, purchase a small blow-torch from a good kitchenware shop and use this to caramelise the sugar. (If grilling, watch carefully to avoid burning the sugar).

500g/16oz (approx.) plum pudding (purchased)
1.1ltr/38fl oz fresh cream
100g/3¹/₄oz powder sugar
225g/8oz dark chocolate
8 large egg yolks
1 tablespoon Dutch cocoa
100g/3¹/₄oz confectioners sugar

Note: Chocolate creme brulee is one of the most seductive desserts you can make. The rich flavours of chocolate and the smooth texture of the custard is enhanced by the crisp toffee coating on top. To celebrate Christmas, I have added the added luxury of a layer of plum pudding on the bottom. Don't wait for Christmas to enjoy this lovely recipe.

Serves 10-12   **Preparation** 30mins   **Cooking** 2hrs rest + 30mins
Calories 780   **Fat** 45g

muddy puddles

85g/3oz chocolate digestive biscuits

85g/3oz butter

85g/3oz plain chocolate

2 tbsp golden syrup

1 medium egg, beaten

few drops of vanilla essence

15g/½oz white chocolate

1 Place the biscuits into a plastic bag, seal, then crush with a rolling pin. Melt 30g /1oz of the butter in a saucepan. Remove from the heat and mix in the biscuits. Line a muffin tin with 4 paper muffin cases. Divide the biscuit mixture between them, pressing over the base and sides of each case with the back of a teaspoon. Refrigerate for 20 minutes or until firm.

2 Preheat the oven to 180°C /350°F/Gas Mark 4. Meanwhile, place the remaining butter, plain chocolate and syrup into a bowl set over a saucepan of simmering water. Heat gently, stirring, until melted. Remove from the heat and cool for 5 minutes. Whisk in the egg and vanilla essence.

3 Spoon the chocolate mixture over the biscuit bases and bake for 20 minutes or until just firm. Leave to cool for 10 minutes. Meanwhile, melt the white chocolate in a bowl set over a pan of simmering water, then drizzle over the puddles.

Note: Chocoholic children (or adults) will adore these pools of chocolate. They've got a chocolate biscuit base, a creamy chocolate filling and even more drizzled on top. Heaven!

Serves 4   **Preparation** 20mins plus 20mins chilling and 15mins cooling
Cooking 25mins   **Calories** 397   **Fat** 28g

chocolate

bread and butter pudding

Serves *4* ***Preparation*** *20 mins* + *10mins standing* ***Cooking*** *40 mins*
Calories *348* ***Fat*** *17g*

15g/¹/₂oz butter

200g/7oz day-old fruit
bread or currant bread,
sliced

2 tbsp chocolate and
hazelnut spread

2 large eggs

285mL/10fl oz
half-fat milk

3 tbsp double cream

1 tbsp sugar (optional)

3 drops vanilla essence

confectioners sugar
to dust

1 Preheat the oven to 180°C/350°F/Gas Mark 4. Use a little of the butter to grease a 23x15cm/9x6in ovenproof baking dish.

2 Cover one side of each bread slice with chocolate spread and cut into triangles if large. Layer the bread, chocolate-side up, in the dish and dot with the remaining butter.

3 Beat the eggs, then beat in the milk, cream, sugar, if using, and vanilla essence. Pour over the bread and leave to stand for 10 minutes before baking. Cook for 35-40 minutes, until well risen and slightly crispy on top. Lightly dust with confectioners sugar.

Note: If you like bread and butter pudding and you like chocolate, you'll love this. For a change, use panettone – the Italian Christmas bread – instead of fruit bread.

chocolate soufflé

30g/1oz unsalted butter, plus extra for greasing

145g/5oz plain chocolate, broken into chunks

6 large eggs, separated

85g/3oz powder sugar

2 tbsp cornstarch

225mL/8fl oz full-fat milk

confectioners sugar to dust

1 Place a baking sheet in the oven and preheat to 200°C/400°F/Gas Mark 6. Lightly butter a 1½ litre/2¾pint soufflé dish. Melt the chocolate with the butter in a bowl placed over a saucepan of simmering water.

2 Whisk the egg yolks and sugar in a large bowl until pale and fluffy. Blend the cornstarch with 1 tablespoon of the milk. Heat the remaining milk in a pan, add the cornflour mixture and bring to the boil, stirring. Cook for 1 minute or until thickened. Remove from the heat and stir into the egg mixture with the melted chocolate, combining thoroughly.

3 Whisk the egg whites until they form stiff peaks (this is best done with an electric whisk). Fold a spoonful of egg white into the chocolate mixture to loosen, then gently fold in the rest. Spoon into the dish and place on the heated baking sheet. Cook for 35 minutes or until well risen. Dust with confectioners sugar and serve immediately.

Serves 4   *Preparation* 20mins   *Cooking* 40mins   *Calories* 518   *Fat* 27g

little pots
of chocolate

2 x 100g/3½oz bars luxury continental plain chocolate, broken into squares

145mL/5fl oz milk

2 tbsp brandy

1 egg

2 egg yolks

1 tsp natural vanilla extract

285mL/10fl oz carton double cream

2 tbsp powder sugar

4 tbsp Greek yoghurt

grated nutmeg to decorate

1 Preheat the oven to 160°C/325°F/Gas Mark 3. Place the chocolate, milk and brandy in a small saucepan. Cook over a low heat, stirring occasionally, for 5-6 minutes, until just melted – do not allow it to boil. Remove from the heat.

2 In a bowl, beat the egg, egg yolks, vanilla extract, cream and sugar until combined. Quickly add to the chocolate mixture, mixing until smooth.

3 Divide the mixture evenly between 4x200mL/7fl oz ramekins. Place on a double layer of newspaper in a baking pan and pour in just enough boiling water to reach halfway up the sides of the dishes. Bake for 35-40 minutes or until lightly set. Remove and leave to cool for 30 minutes, then place in the fridge for 1 hour. Top with the yogurt and grated nutmeg to serve.

Serves 4   **Preparation** 15mins plus 30mins cooling and 1hr chilling
Cooking 45mins   **Calories** 751   **Fat** 98g

285mL/10fl oz
full-fat milk

55g/2oz soft dark
brown sugar

30g/1oz cocoa powder,
sifted

100g/3 1/2oz plain
chocolate, broken into
small chunks

145mL/5fl oz carton
whipping or double
cream

fresh mint to decorate

dark chocolate ice-cream

1 Place the milk and sugar in a saucepan and bring to the boil, then quickly stir in the cocoa powder and add the chocolate chunks. Remove from the heat and stir until the chocolate melts. Set aside to cool for 20 minutes.

2 Whip the cream until it forms soft peaks. Fold it into the warm chocolate mixture and stir gently until thoroughly combined. Pour into a freezer container and freeze for 4 hours or until firm, whisking the mixture every hour. Serve in scoops, decorated with the mint leaves.

Note: Home-made ice creams are delicious, and this is one of the best.
You can make it a week or two in advance, but defrost for 20 minutes before serving, to let it soften.

Serves 4 **Preparation** 10mins plus 20mins cooling and 4hrs freezing
Cooking 5mins **Calories** 377 **Fat** 25g

the cookie
collection

chocolate
and date

1 Preheat the oven to 190°C/370°F/Gas Mark 5. First, make the syrup. Bring all the syrup ingredients to a simmer in a small saucepan, stirring until the sugar dissolves. Continue simmering for 1 minute then cool completely.

2 Next, make the filling. Combine the walnuts, almonds, chocolate, dates, sugar and cinnamon in a food processor, and process until roughly chopped. (Do not over process.) Transfer the mixture to a bowl and mix in the beaten egg.

3 Butter a 30cmx20cm metal baking dish. Unwrap the filo pastry and place it on a flat work surface under a damp cloth. Melt the butter.

4 Place 1 sheet of pastry in front of you then brush lightly with butter, paying particular attention to the edges of the sheet of pastry. Place another sheet of pastry on top of the first, repeating the buttering. Repeat with 6 more sheets so that you have 8 in all. Fold this pastry stack in half to make it fit perfectly into the prepared baking tin, placing it in the tin neatly. Sprinkle half the prepared nut filling over the pastry, taking care to make sure the coverage is even.

5 Repeat the buttering and folding with 8 more sheets of pastry and place the folded pastry over the nuts. Add the remaining nut filling over the second stack of pastry. Repeat the buttering and folding with the remaining sheets of pastry and place over the nut filling.

6 Using a sharp knife, score the pastry into four long strips, then cut these strips diagonally to form 24 diamond-shaped pieces of baklava. Pour any remaining butter over the pastry, then bake for 40 minutes (until the top of the pastry is deep golden brown). Pour the syrup over the baklava then allow to cool completely.

7 Grate the remaining chocolate over the baklava, then allow to stand at room temperature overnight.

Serve with whipped fresh cream (if desired).

stuffed baklava

For the syrup

1 cup white sugar

1/2 cup brown sugar

2/3 cup water

pinch of ground allspice

pinch of ground ginger

pinch of ground cloves

For filling

200g/7oz walnuts, toasted

100g/3 1/2oz almonds, toasted

170g/6oz dark chocolate, chopped

170g/6oz dates, stones removed

2 tablespoons sugar

1 tablespoon cinnamon

1 egg, beaten

1 pack filo pastry, about 24 sheets

55g/2oz chocolate, chopped

double cream, if desired

almond

and white

Serves 10   **Preparation** 30mins   **Cooking** 30mins   **Calories** 336   **Fat** 18g

chocolate macaroons

200g/7½oz marzipan

1 cup powder sugar

2 large egg whites

½ cup toasted, flaked almonds

¼ cup double cream

40g/1⅓oz unsalted butter

grated zest of an orange, grated

170g/6oz white chocolate,chopped

1 tablespoon confectioners sugar

1 Preheat the oven to 175°C/350°F/Gas Mark 5.

2 Generously butter two large non-stick baking trays and set aside.

3 Process the marzipan, castor sugar and egg whites in processor until smooth and thick, then spoon tablespoons of the mixture onto prepared trays, making the mixture into finger size lengths, (rather than rounds). If you prefer, drop spoonfuls onto the tray in rounds. Leave space around each cookie. Sprinkle some flaked, toasted almonds onto each cookie, then bake for 10 minutes or until the cookies are golden brown. Let the cookies cool on the oven trays for 5 minutes then using a spatula, transfer the cookies to a rack and cool completely.

4 Heat the cream, butter and orange zest to a simmer in small saucepan then add the chopped white chocolate and stir until mixture is smooth. Remove from the heat and let the white chocolate cream cool until thick but spreadable, about 15 minutes.

5 When the cookies are completely cold, spread some white chocolate filling over the flat side of a cookie then sandwich with another cookie. Repeat with the remaining cookies and filling then store in an airtight container.

Dust with a little confectioners sugar before serving.

1 Using an electric mixer, cream the butter with the brown sugar until the mixture is light and fluffy then beat in the egg and the vanilla.

2 Sift together the flour, the baking powder and the salt and beat the dough until it is firm enough to handle. Halve the dough then roll each half into a 15cm/6in. log. Wrap each log in a piece of baking paper or plastic wrap and use the paper or plastic to help you roll a tight and even log.

3 Chill the logs, wrapped in the wax paper or plastic for at least 4 hours or overnight.

4 Preheat the oven to 180°C/350°F/Gas Mark 4

5 Cut the logs into 5mm/2in thick slices with a sharp knife and arrange the slices on lightly greased baking trays, leaving plenty of room for spreading. Before baking, press a pecan half onto each cookie.

6 Bake the cookies in batches in the middle of the oven for 10 to 12 minutes, or until they are golden, brown, then let them cool on the baking trays for 1 minute.

7 Repeat the cutting and baking with the remaining dough then transfer all the cookies to racks and let them cool completely.

8 To make the ganache, break the chocolate into small pieces and heat the cream until almost boiling. Pour the hot cream over the chocolate and allow the chocolate to melt slowly. After five minutes, mix the chocolate cream mixture until the chocolate has melted and the mixture is thick and smooth.

9 Leave the chocolate mixture at room temperature until it is spreadable and cool, then fill a piping bag and pipe or spoon a small mound of chocolate ganache onto half of the biscuits. Press another biscuit onto the chocolate, pressing gently to squash the chocolate filling.

10 Allow the cookies and filling to cool and set then serve or store in the fridge for up to 5 days.

Serves 10   **Preparation** 30mins   **Cooking** 12mins   **Calories** 616   **Fat** 28g

pecan thins

370g/13oz unsalted butter, softened	1 1/2 tsp vanilla	about 48 pecan halves
1 cup firmly packed light brown sugar	1 1/2 cups plain flour	100g/3 1/2g good quality dark chocolate
1 large egg	3/4 tsp baking powder	100g/3 1/2fl oz pure cream
	1/2 tsp salt	

sweet little bonfire

115g/4oz dried mixed fruit

55g/2oz corn flakes

100g/3½oz) shredded wheat cookies, crushed (about 4 cookies)

100g/3⅓oz glacé cherries, chopped

170mL/6fl oz condensed milk

145g/5oz desiccated coconut

145g/5oz milk chocolate

1 Preheat the oven to 160°C/325°F/Gas Mark 3. Line 3 baking trays with baking or rice paper. Combine the dried mixed fruit, corn flakes, shredded wheat, cherries, condensed milk and coconut in a large bowl. Press the mixture into little mounds and place on the baking trays, spacing them evenly. Bake for 15 minutes or until golden and crisp.

2 Meanwhile, melt the chocolate in a bowl placed over a saucepan of simmering water. Remove the 'bonfires' from the oven and leave for 2 minutes to cool slightly. Drizzle over the melted chocolate and cool for a further 1-2 minutes before serving.

Note: These are great to hand around on Bonfire Night, and can be made by children without too much supervision. But be warned, they'll disappear faster than a rocket!

caramel squares

For Base

100g/3½oz white melting chocolate

115g/4oz butter

85g/3oz confectioners sugar

55g/2oz macadamia nuts (roasted and ground)

200g/7oz plain flour

For Topping

400g/14oz can sweetened condensed milk

200g/7oz milk chocolate (suitable for melting,)

2 large eggs

2 tbsp plain flour

85g/3oz shortbread biscuits (chopped; but not crushed)

200g/7oz roasted macadamia nuts (roughly chopped)

55g/2oz roasted macadamia nuts (extra)

1 Preheat oven to 180°C/360°F/Gas Mark 4 and grease and line a standard lamington tin (28x18cm/11x7in).

2 First, make the base. Melt the white chocolate then add to a mixer with the butter, icing sugar, crushed macadamia nuts and plain flour.

3 Mix on low speed until all the ingredients are combined, then press the mixture into the prepared tin. Bake for 18 minutes, then cool.

4 Meanwhile, make the topping. In a saucepan, heat the condensed milk and milk chocolate together (until the chocolate has melted). Add the eggs, flour, shortbread biscuit pieces and chopped macadamia nuts, and mix gently.

5 Pour this mixture over the base, then sprinkle extra macadamia nuts over. Bake at 160°C/340°F for 40 minutes.

Remove from the oven and cool completely in the refrigerator before slicing.

Makes 18 squares

techniques

Making Chocolate Leaves, Curls and Shells

Dress up cakes and tortes with chocolate leaves and curls. Fll the shells with white chocolate mousse.

Leaves

Choose thick, waxy no-toxic plant leaves with visible veins such as rose leaves. Brush melted chocolate evenly on underside of leaves. Chill in refrigerator until chocolate is firm. Slide fingernail between leaf and chocolate near stem to loosen chocolate. Pull leaf away from chocolate.

Curls

Use a 4oz/115g or larger bar of chocolate (at room temperature). Scrape the long side of the bar with a sharp vegetable peeler. If chocolate is just the right temperature, you will have nice chocolate curls. If chocolate is too cold, you will end up with short chocolate shavings or shredded chocolate.

Shells

Cover the backs of two 5in/12½cm scallop shells with a layer of plastic film and then layer of foil, pressing foil firmly against ridges. Lightly brush foil with oil and place on baking sheet. Melt chocolate in the top of a double boiler. Spoon melted chocolate over the shells, smoothing with a knife. Store in a cool place until hard (at least 2 hours). Carefully separate chocolate shells from foil and plastic, then trim edges.

Making Chocolate Ruffles and Ribbons

With a little practice you can make chocolate ruffles and ribbons for decorating tortes.

1. For ruffles, refrigerate a marble slab or baking sheet for 30 minutes. Pour an inch-wide 2½cm/1in strip of tempered chocolate onto chilled marble and spread into a thin, smooth sheet 3x10in/7½ x 25cm.

2. When chocolate begins to set but is still pliable, use a spatula to push sheet of chocolate from right to left. With left hand gather chocolate into a ruffle as you go along. Transfer ruffle to a pan lined with waxed paper, cover with plastic wrap, and refrigerate until ready to use. Make enough ruffles to decorate top of torte.

3. For ribbon, cut a sheet of waxed paper slightly wider than the cake is tall and slightly longer than the cake's circumference. With a spatula, spread a thin layer of melted, tempered chocolate onto the waxed paper. When the chocolate begins to set but is still pliable, place one end of the ribbon of chocolate against the cake, with layer of chocolate facing in, and wrap smoothly against sides of cake. Press top edge on chocolate ribbon onto top of cake. Refrigerate until firm and waxed paper pulls away easily.

index